THE ROWMAN & LITTLEFIELD GUIDE TO WRITING WITH SOURCES

JAMES P. DAVIS

ROWMAN & LITTLEFIELD PUBLISHERS, INC.
Lanham•Boulder•New York•Oxford

ROWMAN & LITTLEFIELD PUBLISHERS, INC.

Published in the United States of America
by Rowman & Littlefield Publishers, Inc.
4720 Boston Way, Lanham, Maryland 20706
www.rowmanlittlefield.com

12 Hid's Copse Road
Cumnor Hill, Oxford OX2 9JJ, England

British Library Cataloguing in Publication Information Available

Library of Congress Cataloging-in-Publication Data

Davis, James P., 1954–
 The Rowman & Littlefield guide to writing with sources / James P. Davis.
  p. cm.
 Includes bibliographical references.
 ISBN 0-7425-1842-6 (alk. paper)
 1. English language—Rhetoric—Handbooks, manuals, etc. 2. Research—Methodology—Handbooks, manuals, etc. 3. Report writing—Handbooks, manuals, etc. I. Title: Rowman and Littlefield guide to writing with sources. II. Title.

PE1478 .D37 2002
808'.0042'072—dc21   2001057859

Printed in the United States of America

♾™ The paper used in this publication meets the minimum requirements of American National Standard for Information Sciences—Permanence of Paper for Printed Library Materials, ANSI/NISO Z39.48-1992.

CONTENTS

INTRODUCTION

Writing that matters is both informed and informative. Your reader, whether a professor, a student, or a broader group, expects your writing to have authority—a mix of confidence, clear purpose, and relevant information. As you craft your writing to meet these needs, you will frequently need to consult published information and opinions. Information has never been so abundant and readily available. But as kinds and quantities of sources have proliferated, it has become crucial to read all publications critically. Such reading involves essential intellectual skills, as you assess the relationship of the information you have found to your project, evaluate its credibility and relevance, select the best use of the material, represent it accurately and fairly, and fully and coherently integrate it into your project. You must also acknowledge and cite the sources you have used in a methodical and clear way. Whether you quote them or paraphrase the information you have found; whether they are published books, unsigned articles, or documents found on the Internet; and whether your project is a formal report or a personal essay, you must clearly signal that you have employed these resources and learn to cite them in ways that are ethical, precise, rhetorically effective, and consistent with practices established for the field in which you are writing.

DECISIONS TO MAKE

When you wish to use some information you've found or to quote a viewpoint that is expressed in some source, you need to make a number of decisions.

- Do you need to acknowledge the source of your information?
- Should you paraphrase or quote the material?
- If quoting, how much of the passage should you reproduce in your paper?
- How should you introduce and present the material?
- How should you make the transition to the quoted material and then back to your own prose so that your readers will always understand the status of the words they are reading?
- How should you cite electronic and Internet sources?

This book will help you to answer these questions.

PLAGIARISM

The writing skills involved in using quotations or information from sources are basic ones that you will be expected to employ in all of your college writing. Your ability to use sources ethically and clearly is crucial to your success in every course, in any major you pursue, in whatever profession you choose. Yet beginning college students often arrive at college without these basic skills. The purpose of this book is to enable you to incorporate quoted or paraphrased material into your writing in ways that credit the sources you consult for wording or ideas that are not your own and that will permit your audience to comprehend your ideas and to have confidence in your authority as a writer. Mastering the skills discussed here will broaden your options as you write, increase your confidence as a student, and empower you to write with clarity and authority. Neglecting these skills will cripple your abilities to communicate and, worse, in some cases, render you vulnerable to charges of academic dishonesty.

Sometimes, if students are having a particularly stressful semester, they mistakenly believe that if they lift some ideas or phrases from someone else's work, they've found an easy way to meet an impending deadline. Or in their haste to complete some work on which they've procrastinated, they allow themselves to take such sloppy notes that they use ideas or phrasing from a source without citing it properly. In English classes, for example, they may feel that they can borrow unacknowledged ideas from *Cliffs* or *Monarch Notes* about a work of literature they are discussing. Or they might copy material from the work of another student or reuse a paper they wrote in a prior class without first discussing it with the professor. The World Wide Web has produced its own set of temptations to students. It might not seem like cheating when all one has to do is point and click to find some ready-made phrasing, without even needing to transcribe it. But all of these are forms of serious academic dishonesty that—students are often surprised to learn—instructors detect easily. Instructors are familiar with the capabilities of most students and sensitive to features of individual students' writing styles. They are also familiar with the published work in their fields, well trained to recognize the contributions of professional writers. A variety of specialized search engines and online services enable instructors to locate the original sources of wording and ideas stolen from published and electronic sources—often more quickly than the student was able to find them in the first place. Plagiarism has never been so easy—but it has never been so easy to detect. No one enjoys being suspicious, and no task is more abhorrent to an instructor than confronting a dishonest or careless student and proceeding with judicial action. It is far more satisfying to work with students to train them to use sources responsibly before questions about their integrity arise. You must do your part to make certain that you understand the material and apply it whenever you write a paper. Don't let the fear of misusing quoted material dissuade you from doing research. Instead, master the skills of quoting and paraphrasing responsibly, confident that, when you do so, you will gain a powerful and indispensable skill.

POPULAR STYLE MANUALS

This book does not present comprehensive formats for listing different kinds of sources, because different disciplines follow different conventions for citing sources. A book or pamphlet that presents a specific format is called a style manual. Some commonly used style manuals include the following:

1. Modern Language Association's *MLA Handbook for Writers of Research Papers*, for English and modern languages
2. Turabian's *Manual for Writers of Term Papers, Theses, and Dissertations*, for history and other humanities (based on the *Chicago Manual of Style*)
3. *Scientific Style and Format*, published by the Council of Biology Editors (CBE), for biological sciences
4. *Publication Manual of the American Psychological Association* (APA), for psychology
5. *Handbook for Authors*, published by the American Chemical Society, for chemistry
6. *Style Manual for Political Science*, published by the American Political Science Association (APSA), for political science

Because my discipline is English, the examples that follow will be based on the format presented in the *MLA Handbook*. You may need to follow a different format. Ask your professor or your editor which style manual to use. Consult it to find out how to present your references. Your college library probably has copies of all of the style manuals mentioned, and most are available online. You would be wise to purchase the style manual preferred by your discipline as soon as you declare your major. If your professor does not specify a particular style manual or referencing format, you are not freed from the responsibility of referencing information you take from other sources, nor are you free to make up your own format. You still need to follow one of the published style manuals.

Whatever style manual you use for a particular course or paper, remember that the purpose of all of them is threefold:

1. To help you establish your authority and provide documentation for your claims in a systematic way
2. To help you provide your readers with all of the information they need to find your original sources and verify your claims about them

3. To provide a system for briefly identifying a source in your text with minimum textual clutter in ways that clearly refer to the fully cited work in a list at the end

ELEMENTS REQUIRED IN A CITATION

Even before you begin to gather information and take notes for a project, you need to know what sorts of information about the source you need in order to cite it properly—both in your list of works cited and in those portions of your text where you have used it.

If you are taking information from a book, all style manuals demand that you include in the final list:

- author
- title
- volume number (if a multivolume work)
- date of publication
- place of publication
- publisher
- page number(s)

Within your text itself, you may need to provide only the author's last name and the page number (or, for some disciplines, a year of publication). If you have used only one work by that author, it will be clear to which work in the list the name refers.

For articles, your works cited list must include:

- author
- title of article
- title of journal or magazine
- volume and issue numbers
- date
- page number(s)

As you do with books, in your text itself you should keep your information about a source as brief as you can, providing just enough information to enable your reader to identify the full citation in your works cited list at the end. You refer to the full citation with the author's name (if known) or with an abbreviated title of the article (if the author is not known), and the page number.

Internet sources may or may not name their authors, and they won't have conventional page numbers. But you should provide the name of the author or organization (if it is available) or the title of the site (typically abbreviated for your in-text references), taking care to provide in your list of works cited the entire electronic address (or URL) and the date you accessed it. When you take notes, make sure that you distinguish carefully between quoted words and your own words, and note the page number of print sources from which the information was taken. Copy all of the necessary information (as specified above) that would allow someone else to locate that same source. Spare yourself the need to return to the library simply to find the name of the publisher or the page number from which a certain quotation or paraphrased information came. *One further caution*: It is not adequate merely to list a work you have used in your works cited. You must at all times make certain that it is clear what portion of the cited source has been used in your work.

This book presents ways to select and incorporate source material into your work that are shared by all disciplines. Get into the habit now of employing the following suggestions. You will find that all of your writing will be stronger.

WHEN DO YOU NEED TO ACKNOWLEDGE A SOURCE?

Some of what you write will come from your own observations and experience, some from class notes and discussion, some from what we call "common knowledge," some from the assigned readings in the course, some from works you've sought out on your own. Each of these sources merits a bit of discussion.

Obviously, you need not document in any formal way your own observations or experiences. The power of your own written voice should convince your readers of the plausibility of your own ideas and experiences.

MATERIAL FROM CLASSROOM DISCUSSION

In most circumstances, you are free to incorporate ideas that have been explored in class discussion without worrying about the ownership of those ideas. Usually you may feel free to draw on background information presented in class as you provide a context for the more focused and developed discussion in your paper. If the class lecture or discussion itself has drawn on sources, such as films or readings, then you should attribute relevant ideas to their original source. But instructors do not expect or desire credit in your paper for ideas generated in class. Two suggestions:

1. Your own paper should probably not consist entirely of ideas repeated from class; instead, it should develop ideas more fully or apply them in

new ways that demonstrate your understanding of them. Ask your instructor for suggestions if you are concerned that your paper may simply rehash ideas presented in class.

2. When you do rely on ideas or information from class, remember to explain them fully. Think of your audience as a group of people who are
intelligent but who have not attended class. Anyone who picks up your
paper should be able to understand it—not just the professor for whom
you have written the paper.

COMMON KNOWLEDGE

The category of information we call "common knowledge" is a more complex
matter. Common knowledge includes broad historical facts that are not the conclusions or discoveries of a particular author, for example the fact that John
Kennedy was the 35th president of the United States, or that Emily Brontë died
the year after *Wuthering Heights* was published, or that under normal atmo-
spheric pressure, water boils at 100° Celsius. Even if you have to look up
common-knowledge facts like these in a reference work, you do not need to cite
your source. Nor do you have to document commonly known generalizations,
such as the assumption that the Romantic Era in British literature was a time of
intense literary innovation, or that computers have revolutionized communication, or that laboratory experimentation with animals is controversial. When you
are beginning your studies of a particular subject, you might not always be able
to tell easily what is common knowledge within a discipline and what isn't. But
as you read more widely in a field with an eye toward what the other authors assume is shared information, you will be better able to assess what information
properly belongs to particular authors. Two cautions:

1. Even if you judge a bit of information to be shared publicly, be careful
not to represent another writer's phrasing of this common knowledge
as your own. Although the information may be common knowledge, a
specific writer's expression of the information is still the property of
that writer.

2. If you cannot decide if some information needs to be credited to an author, provide a reference giving credit. When in doubt, cite your source.

Common knowledge also includes traditional tales, folk literature, and folk wisdom—tales or observations that are handed down without knowledge of who wrote the tale or made the observation. Many fairy tales—for instance, those of Mother Goose—or age-old songs and jokes—such as "Three Blind Mice" and "Why did the chicken cross the road?"—do not require documentation of the source. Nor would you need to provide a note crediting some source with the observation that a dog is man's best friend, that absence makes the heart grow fonder, or that a bird in the hand is worth two in the bush. Many clichés or sayings fall into this category, though where authors are known, you should mention them. You should, for example, acknowledge that it was Alexander Pope who wrote "To err is human, to forgive divine," or Thomas Paine who wrote "These are the times that try men's souls." But generalized, commonsense observations do not usually need to be credited to a source. Be forewarned, however, that most readers will not continue reading something that tells them things they already know, and they will probably be irritated if your phrasing is hackneyed or your observations trite. If you use clichés in formal writing, use them in some fresh or unexpected way, or your readers will probably assume that you have nothing new to say and may lose interest.

USING TEXTBOOKS AS SOURCES

When you draw on information from a course textbook or from a source you have found on your own, you need to credit the source for all information drawn from it that is not common knowledge. For informal papers in which you refer only to class textbooks, professors may not demand that you give a complete reference that includes all of the publication facts. Ask your professor if it is acceptable merely to specify the author and title, and put the page number from which the information was taken in parentheses at the end of the sentence. Even if the source is a class textbook and the author and title are clear from the context (the assignment is a paper on *Wuthering Heights*, for example), you must at least cite the edition and page number because your professor will want to be able to locate the exact page from which you are getting the information, whether you quote it directly or paraphrase it. Even when you are writing a short "homework" or in-class assignment, you should acknowledge material that is not your own. You should provide proper citations of your sources not merely to avoid plagiarism, but to empower your writing with authority, evidence, and illustrative detail.

WHEN SHOULD YOU PARAPHRASE AND WHEN SHOULD YOU QUOTE?

Done properly, paraphrasing information gives you remarkable flexibility and, by permitting you to select only the information most relevant to your topic, it enables you to express your ideas with a minimum of verbiage. In short, it ensures that all of the information is pertinent, and it helps you to write with economy and vigor. When readers encounter information paraphrased or summarized from one of your sources, they do not have to move between writing by you and that by another author, shifting to a new voice, a new style, a different pace and context. When you paraphrase well, you do your reader a great service, because you've selected, organized, and phrased the information to suit your purposes, all in a manner that preserves a continuity of style and emphasis. But paraphrasing requires more work of you than simply copying someone else's words.

TO PARAPHRASE OR TO QUOTE?

It is appropriate for you to paraphrase, instead of quoting, whenever the wording itself is less important to the purpose of your writing than the information it presents. If all you need from an economic study, for example, is the distressing information that, nationally, a woman with a college degree has the same earning potential as a male high school dropout, simply paraphrase the conclusions of the study in your own words and state your source, rather than quoting the study. Citing a statistic, a relatively unknown fact, a bit of information embedded in a study that otherwise is not relevant to your topic—in all of these situations, it is advisable to paraphrase rather than to quote. Conversely, if the source itself is important to your topic, if the original wording helps you to illustrate your point, if the opinion expressed in the passage is controversial or highly unusual, or if the work itself *is* your subject (as in a paper on a literary work), then it is advisable to quote the actual words the original author used.

THE POWER OF VERBATIM SOURCE MATERIAL

The next time you watch a televised news program, notice how the news writers use sources to establish the credibility of their reporting. The orchestrated movements to and from different locations, to and from other correspondents, other cameras and voices—these movements are analogous to an author's presentation of information in nonfiction writing. If they chose to, news anchors could present all of the news stories in their (or their news editor's) own words. Actually, doing so would provide better quality of both visual images and recorded language than the grainy, sometimes poorly focused film footage that is shot by foreign correspondents with their handheld cameras in the heat of battle. Many news anchors do present much of the information themselves, particularly economic news (which doesn't film very dramatically) or stories for which they have no taped footage. But roughly half of the time, they turn the story over to a person in the field, to an eyewitness speaking without revising, or to a correspondent who narrates over some film footage, blurred by the processes of photography, distanced by the satellite transmission. Why? The answer is probably obvious. Going to the sources that are close to the story, to the people who are more authoritative than the anchors themselves, contributes to their credibility. The news anchors become more authoritative for knowing when to let someone else be the authority. They introduce the news item and the taped footage, they let us know who is speaking, then they show us the tape, frequently following the segment with some kind of concluding remarks to give the story a sense of closure. Any edition of the evening news will demonstrate a similar use of primary source material. Even though the conventions of video documentation differ from those of printed writing—for example, there are no footnotes in a newscast—the purpose of such material is evident.

Paraphrase (with proper citations) when all you need is the information itself.

Quote when your source is important, when you can gain authority by turning to another author.

HOW SHOULD YOU PARAPHRASE INFORMATION FROM A SOURCE?

Once you've decided that the occasion calls for paraphrasing, you need to do several things.

SELECTING INFORMATION FROM YOUR SOURCE

First, you need to select the information relevant to your topic and make certain that you completely rephrase the ideas—in your own words. Do not use any phrases, syntax, or organization that appeared in the original work. These are the author's personal property, and representing segments or features of a passage as your own constitutes plagiarism.

An Example of Paraphrasing

Suppose you are writing a paper on blue jeans as a cultural phenomenon, exploring what the enduring popularity of blue jeans illustrates about our culture. You find an essay in *American Heritage*, "The Jeaning of America—and the World," by Carin Quinn, in which she writes the following about Levi's jeans (on page 18):

> The pants have become a tradition, and along the way have acquired a history of their own—so much so that the company has opened a museum in San

Francisco. There was, for example, the turn-of-the-century trainman who replaced a faulty coupling with a pair of jeans; the Wyoming man who used his jeans as a towrope to haul his car out of a ditch; the Californian who found several pairs in an abandoned mine, wore them, then discovered they were sixty-three years old and still as good as new and turned them over to the Smithsonian as a tribute to their toughness. And then there is the particularly terrifying story of the careless construction worker who dangled fifty-two stories above the street until rescued, his sole support the Levi's belt loop through which his rope was hooked.

You decide that the information about the museum and her examples of heroically strong jeans would strengthen your argument about what the jeans symbolize, and you write the following:

> The jeans have earned a history all their own—to such an extent that the Levi's corporation even operates a museum of jeans in San Francisco. The museum presents the stories of the trainman who hitched two trains together with a pair of jeans, of the Wyoming man who towed his car out of a ditch using a pair of the jeans, of the Californian who found several pairs in an abandoned mine, put them on, discovered they were still good as new after sixty-three years, and donated them to the Smithsonian as a tribute to their toughness. One especially horrifying story is that of the construction worker who lost his footing and dangled some fifty stories over the street, hanging only from the Levi's belt loop which his rope was hooked on. [improper paraphrase—plagiarism]

If you left this paragraph in your paper—even if you provided a note naming Carin Quinn as your source, and even if you didn't intend to deceive anyone— you would be guilty of plagiarism. Even though much of the paragraph has been rephrased, much of it hasn't been. This paragraph is organized exactly like the original, and much of the rewriting is merely substitution of synonyms for her original words, relying far too heavily on her syntax. The phrase "particularly terrifying," for example, is replaced by "especially horrifying," with much of the original sentence left intact. The exact repetition of "found several pairs in an abandoned mine" and of the phrase "tribute to their toughness" is especially damning. If this wording is important enough to repeat verbatim, then you should quote it; otherwise, the passage should be completely reworded.

A far better example of paraphrasing, one that incorporates Quinn's ideas into the author's own argument, would be the following use of the material:

Every morning, as you slip into your jeans, you put on a part of American history. You might merely be seeking warmth on a cold day or trying to make yourself decent for a walk downtown, but your jeans bring with them a long cultural tradition and probably more legendary strength than you'll ever need to run your errands. According to Carin Quinn, a pair of the original Levi's served once as a rope for a man in Wyoming who needed to tow his car from a ditch. A trainman once used a pair of the jeans to couple together two railway cars when its original coupling had broken. And when a hapless construction worker lost his footing fifty-two stories above the earth, one loop of his jeans was sufficient to hold him until help arrived (18). The Levi's corporation is well aware of its image. The leather patch with the Levi trademark shows a pair of jeans pulled between two horses. Most days you probably won't be repairing trains, dangling overhead, or deliberately frustrating the movement of horses, but wearing blue jeans symbolically connects you with the strength, ingenuity, preparedness, and even heroism embodied in these legends about the jeans.

Granted, this paragraph contains many ideas not found in the original source. And Quinn's paragraph presents information not included in this passage. But that's part of the point. You shouldn't simply repeat ideas you've found elsewhere; you should incorporate those ideas into a context all your own. And you should make clear which of the ideas in the paragraph derive from Quinn's work and which are entirely your own. Including the author's name at the beginning and a page or note number (depending on your style manual) at the end of the paraphrased material makes it clear which information came from another source and which didn't. When you do find some useful information in a source you've consulted, you should explicitly name the author, select only those details that suit your purpose, phrase them in wording that is entirely your own, provide the page number, and then print the full publishing information in a section entitled "Works Cited" at the end of your paper.

GIVING CREDIT TO YOUR SOURCE

The second thing you must do has already been mentioned but bears repeating here: Even if you are not quoting actual words, you need to give credit for the information, and you need to make clear exactly what has come from your source.

Sometimes students believe that all they need to do if they've drawn information from a source is provide a note number at the end of the paragraph containing the paraphrased material, confident that they've given credit where credit is due. This practice, however, is dangerously ambiguous and even misleading. A numbered note at the end of a paragraph implies that *all* of the material in the paragraph had its origin in the cited source, even if the paragraph is a mix of borrowed information and original insight. This practice might attribute ideas to the cited author that he or she did not develop, and it completely muddies the distinction between your own ideas and the other author's. For example, in the last sample paragraph on jeans, if I had not mentioned the author's name where I did and if I had waited until the end of the paragraph to provide the page (or note) number, I would have inaccurately represented all of the ideas in the paragraph as Quinn's, thereby denying myself credit for the ideas that precede and follow the paraphrased material. Quinn does not make the observation that Levi's represents American ingenuity and preparedness for adversity. That idea is mine, and I shouldn't allow mere sloppiness with writing technique to rob me of credit for the idea. The author's name at the beginning of the paraphrased material and the page number at the end of it function a bit as the beginning and ending quotation marks would if the material were quoted—they set off the cited information from your own, signaling its different status from the other words, identifying the source with maximum clarity and minimal distraction. In short, think of embedding the paraphrased material in your own prose as a kind of linguistic bracketing or fencing off of the information in as clear a way as possible, so as not to give the author too little credit—or too much.

THE IMPORTANCE OF ACCURACY IN PARAPHRASING

Finally, you need to make certain that your synopsis of the author's ideas accurately reflects the author's actual statement. It probably goes without saying that you shouldn't misrepresent a paraphrased source, yet often students seem rather cavalier about restating others' ideas. Notice how frequently letters to the editor in your student newspaper attempt to correct a perceived misreading of an earlier letter. In the heat of the debate about campus issues, people often say things imprecisely and misread the letters of others. Most of your sources are far more carefully composed than such letters. So should be your reading of them. Imagine that the authors whose words you are para-phrasing are going to read your synopsis of what they said. Will they feel that their views have been accurately and fairly represented? You may certainly disagree with what an author says in print, but it only helps to establish your credibility if you present those ideas fairly (maybe even quoting especially pertinent lines), before going on to demonstrate what is wrong with the au-thor's position.

The focus and length of your project should guide you as you decide how much of the source you plan to use. It is usually best not to use only a general or concluding remark as if it is sufficient by itself to constitute evidence or ar-gument. Neglecting to explain the author's reasons for her or his position and simply using a general phrase from the work will make it seem as if you are content to rely on authority assertions rather than to critically assess the ideas. Whether you agree with or challenge the published view (paraphrased or quoted), it helps you to establish your thoroughness and fairness if you at-tend to the reasoning behind an author's conclusions as you use the material.

HOW SHOULD YOU QUOTE MATERIAL FROM A SOURCE?

HOW MUCH TO QUOTE

Students sometimes wonder what proportion of their papers should be quoted material and what should be original words of their own. At one extreme, their papers might consist of lengthy quoted passages, stitched together with a few transitions of their own, as if writing were like assembling a patchwork quilt out of fragments of others' cloth. At the other extreme, students might quote only once, leaving most of their paragraphs without quotations, which serve as illustration or evidence. Either extreme is disproportionate. Think of quoting as a valuable means of developing and supporting ideas—not as the means of presenting the ideas themselves. In some cases, quotations will be the best form your evidence could take, and neglecting to include relevant quotations could mean neglecting to provide convincing illustrative material. When you are revising your paper, read through it once without reading the quoted words. If your paper makes little sense without the quotations, you've probably attempted to make them do too much. *Your* words should present your argument; the quotations are only supportive material—valuable and essential to convincing your reader, but never the primary means of presenting information.

HOW TO PRESENT A QUOTATION

Once you've decided that it is appropriate to quote, you need to decide how much of the passage merits being presented in your paper. It may be that the information you need is entangled in a long sentence or paragraph, most of which is beside your immediate point. In this case, were you to quote the entire sentence or paragraph, you would needlessly divert your readers' attention from your immediate topic. You can quote passages of virtually any length: a word, a phrase, a sentence, even a paragraph. But whatever you quote should be entirely relevant to your purpose, and the longer the passage you quote, the greater should be your use of the material. Most of the time it would be rhetorically ineffective to quote a long passage, unless you plan to analyze or interpret it at some length, following the quotation. In most instances, your task will be to select a phrase or sentence that best illustrates the point you are making and, taking great care to copy the material exactly as it is written, fit the quoted author's words into your own, making certain that you mark the quoted passage with quotation marks; name the source of the material (if it isn't already clear in the paragraph); and work the phrases into your own in a way that produces grammatical and coherent statements.

Never present a quotation as a completely separate sentence. Always introduce it in some way. The presence of quotation marks (without any introduction or transition) is not a sufficient signal that the material has come from a source, because writers use quotation marks for some purposes other than quoting. They might mark a word that they are using in a special way or mark a word that they are discussing. When I mention "common knowledge" above, I put it in quotation marks, because I was discussing what the phrase means. Some authors who need to use a slang expression will surround the expression with quotation marks as if to apologize for using the phrase. It is not a particularly admirable practice, but it is a fairly common one. Don't "fly off the handle" at such practices; instead, keep your "cool." The important point here is to introduce all quotations in ways that indicate you are quoting, that identify the source, and that suggest the significance of what the person is saying.

As you lead into a quoted passage, you should consider what sorts of information about your source the reader needs to know to understand the significance of the quotation.

- Does the author have a position or credentials that are relevant to the quoted statement?
- Is the date of the statement important enough to note as you introduce it?
- Was the quoted passage published originally as a part of a major study?
- Has the author employed a particular research methodology that might contextualize the study within the field?
- Has the author made use of important or unusual materials?
- Is the journal or other medium in which the piece appears particularly noteworthy?

If you know this kind of information and it helps to establish the context of the material within the field of your topic, you should consider including it as you introduce a quoted passage. Think of the reasons that you consulted the source in the first place and the reasons why you selected the passage that you did.

If you can signal these reasons to your reader as you introduce the material, your reader might better understand the relationship of the quoted passage to your essay. At the very least, you should convey that the quoted material comes from a source:

"According to one study . . ."
"One author puts it this way . . ."
"A later report claims that . . ."

Better yet, name the source:

"Miller argues that . . ."
"Johnston, who studied the mosquito for fifteen years, postulates that . . ."
"The chief engineer on the project, Eliza Swaney, observes . . ."

And if the passage is important, alert your reader to the nature of its significance or to its context in your work:

"Jonathan Alder offers a contrasting view . . ."
"Linkholder's rebuttal shows her dependence on Connelly's theorem . . ."
"Note the veiled anger in Cramer's reply . . ."

Your objective is to signal your movements to and from a quotation with max-imum clarity, continuity, and context, and to encourage your reader to predict what will follow in a quotation. As you read authors you admire in the field for which you are writing, get in the habit of noticing how the authors have chosen to do what they do. When you encounter writing done well, read it carefully, not just for the information you need, but to learn from their exam-ple alternate ways of meeting your needs as a writer.

HOW TO SHOW ADDITIONS
AND DELETIONS IN A QUOTATION

Between the opening set of quotation marks and the closing pair, every word, letter, and punctuation mark must be exactly as it appears in the original. You can change some of the things in a quotation—adding or deleting words—but only if you indicate that you have done so and only if your change does not dis-tort the meaning of what you've quoted. One change is permitted—actually re-quired—within a quotation: If the source itself quotes something else, you change the double quotation marks to single ones, so that they are not con-fused with the ones that you have provided. You may also change the final punctuation mark in your quotation of a passage to suit your own grammati-cal needs (see below), in effect stopping your quotation before the final symbol. But if grammar demands that you add a word, change the tense of a quoted verb, or clarify the reference of a quoted pronoun, for instance, you should do so by enclosing your change in square brackets (not parentheses). If you are using a typewriter and it does not have square brackets [or], leave spaces as you type where the brackets should be and write them in neatly in black ink. If for reasons of clarity, grammar, or brevity, you decide to delete a word or phrase from within a series of quoted words, put in its place an ellipsis, three spaced dots enclosed in square brackets [. . .], to show your reader that you've left something out. Periods that you add for this purpose should be enclosed in the square brackets to make it clear that you added them and that they were not in the original work for some other purpose. Space once before the open-ing bracket, *between* the periods themselves, and once after the closing bracket so that your ellipsis looks like this: [. . .] If quoting the passage requires ex-tensive bracketing and ellipses, to the extent that you must undergo all sorts of grammatical or typographic contortions, consider paraphrasing the material or quoting only the most relevant phrases or words. The following examples will illustrate how to use square brackets and the ellipsis.

Assume for the moment that you are writing an essay on F. Scott Fitzgerald's *The Great Gatsby*, exploring the ways in which the narrator, Nick Carraway, is biased as he relates the events. Because your topic is a work of literature, and especially because you are attempting to show how the narrator's language reveals his attitudes, you will frequently wish to quote from the novel. You will find no more direct source of evidence to convince skeptical readers than quoting the actual novel.

Using Square Brackets to Mark Words Added in a Quotation

Original (from page 39 of Fitzgerald's *The Great Gatsby*):
In his blue gardens men and girls came and went like moths among the whisperings and the champagne and the stars.

Your use of the passage (the page number follows the passage):
Nick Carraway, the narrator in the novel, says "In his [Gatsby's] blue gardens men and girls came and went like moths among the whisperings and the champagne and the stars" (39).

Explanation

By itself, the original "his" in the passage would have incorrectly implied that the gardens under discussion were Nick's instead of Gatsby's. In this case, a more graceful way of clarifying the meaning of the pronoun would be to provide a referent for "his" as you introduce the quotation, as in the following:

Early in the novel, Nick reveals his contempt for Gatsby's guests: "In his blue gardens men and girls came and went like moths among the whisperings and the champagne and the stars" (39).

This use of the material avoids the clutter of the brackets and better alerts the reader to notice Nick's judgment of the guests. Yet another way to use this material (and other relevant details from the novel) might be to write the following:

Despite Nick's early claim that he is "inclined to reserve all judgments" (1), he says that Tom has "a cruel body" (7), and he refers to Gatsby's guests as "moths" (39).

This might be an even better use of the material, depending on the focus and context of the essay. It explains why it matters that Nick is in fact judgmental, and it makes use of selected phrases or words that illustrate this trait. Between the pairs of quotation marks, every word is identical to the original. And each quotation is followed by the number of the page on which the passage appears. If you can rework your use of a passage so as to avoid using the brackets, do so. But if you need to change something, employ the brackets to signify that change. Following is one more example of how bracketed information may clarify the meaning of a pronoun. While it is clear in the novel that Nick is speaking of Gatsby in these lines, removing the passage from its context requires that you clarify the meaning in your context.

Original (from page 102):
For several weeks I didn't see him or hear his voice on the phone—mostly I was in New York, trotting around with Jordan and trying to ingratiate myself with her senile aunt—but finally I went over to his house one Sunday afternoon.

Your use of the material:
Nick makes it clear that the only events of that summer that interest him now are those involving Gatsby. At one point he alludes to other events, but he quickly returns to his real subject:

> For several weeks I didn't see him [Gatsby] or hear his voice on the phone—mostly I was in New York, trotting around with Jordan and trying to ingratiate myself with her senile aunt—but finally I went over to his house one Sunday afternoon. (102)

Here Nick summarizes "several weeks" in only nineteen words, those weeks not mattering because they didn't involve his hero, Gatsby.

Explanation

Notice again the simple way you can clear up a potentially confusing pronoun with information enclosed in brackets. Notice also that when the quoted passage is relatively long (more than three typed lines), you present it in "block" format: you set it off from the rest of your text by indenting it. When you present block quotations, you should not enclose the material in quotation marks unless they appear in the original. Setting it off in block format already tells the reader that the material is quoted. The page number or any other parenthetical publication information follows the period at the end of the block quotation. Notice also that the paragraph does not end simply because I presented a block quotation. I followed the passage with attention to its details, connecting it to the idea I'm developing. Beginning and closing lines in paragraphs are positions of extreme emphasis; don't leave your reader dangling at the end of block quotations. Resume your analysis, closing the paragraph by returning to your immediate point.

If your paper is written in the present tense and you wish to quote something written in the past tense, bracket the part of the verb you change:

Original (from page 80):
He had waited five years and bought a mansion where he dispensed starlight to casual moths—so that he could "come over" some afternoon to a stranger's garden.

Your use of the material:
Nick implies throughout the novel that Gatsby's guests are undeserving of his social efforts, saying that Gatsby "dispense[s] starlight to casual moths" (80).

Notice, as always, the quoted material is introduced in some way that makes its source and its importance clear to your reader.

Using the Ellipsis to Indicate That You Deleted Words from a Quotation

If you decide, in the interests of brevity and relevance, to leave out some material from the middle of a quoted passage, provide the ellipsis (three spaced periods) within square brackets to show it. The deletion, obviously, should not change the meaning of the passage, nor should it produce a series of words that do not fit grammatically with the rest of your writing. If you are omitting an entire sentence or more from within a quotation, you should provide the regular period at the end of the sentence before the deleted material, and then provide the usual ellipsis (three spaced periods within square brackets) to show that one or more sentences have been deleted. Do not begin or end a quotation with ellipses. Especially if you are quoting only a word or a phrase, surrounding the quoted material with ellipses only adds unnecessary clutter.

Suppose you are writing an essay on a phenomenon called "grade inflation" in college classes, the trend over the last few decades for instructors to give higher grades to work that would have earned lower grades in decades past. You find a discussion of patterns in grading at Harvard University, written by Craig Lambert, entitled "Desperately Seeking Summa," in *Harvard Magazine* (May–June 1993) and decide to use some of the material from the following passage:

Original (from page 36):
The grade of C, which nominally signifies an "average" performance, has virtually disappeared from Harvard transcripts: last year about 91 percent of undergraduate grades were B– or higher (see graph). D's and E's are virtually extinct. "The five-letter system has gone to three letters," says Katherine Tulenko '93, a biochemistry concentrator and a marshal of the Radcliffe chapter of Phi Beta Kappa. Her fellow PBK marshal, Elaine Goldenberg '93, notes that "a lot of people today would consider a C as equivalent to what a D or even an E used to mean—a very poor grade." Tulenko amplifies: "Ask any student how they would feel about getting a B–. They'll make an ugly face."

Your use of the material:
Apparently grading standards have relaxed even at such rigorous institutions as Harvard. Craig Lambert, an editor at *Harvard Magazine*, reports that "The grade of C [. . .] has virtually disappeared from Harvard transcripts: last year [1992] about 91 percent of undergraduate grades were B– or higher [. . .]. D's and E's are virtually extinct." To gauge student reaction to this phenomenon, Lambert quotes a student officer of Phi Beta Kappa, who reports that "a lot of people today would consider a C as equivalent to what a D or even an E used to mean—a very poor grade" (36).

Explanation

This passage illustrates a variety of things. An ellipsis in square brackets replaces Lambert's explanation that a C denotes an average performance, which might already have been made clear elsewhere in the essay. The graph referred to at the end of Lambert's first sentence in the original has not been reproduced, so it, too, has been replaced with an ellipsis, because the reference will make no sense in the new context. Notice that the usual three spaced dots in brackets are followed by a regular period—one that is outside of the brackets to signify that it is a final punctuation mark for the sentence and not merely part of the ellipsis. Lambert's reference to "last year" would be vague in an essay written several years after his, so the year he refers to has been added (within square brackets) to clarify his meaning and to show that the year was added as the material was quoted. Because the same page of Lambert's essay is used again immediately after the first use, the page number is not presented until the end of the final quotation. It will be clear that both quotations are from the same page. The second quotation from Lambert's essay is actually his quoting of a student, a situation that is mentioned in the text itself. The page number is not part of either quotation but it is part of the sentence, so it is placed after the quotation marks but before the period. In general, select what is relevant and important enough to quote; use the ellipsis within brackets to indicate that you have left out material within the original; use square brackets to designate material added to the original; introduce quoted sources explicitly in your text; make certain that all words (quoted and unquoted) fit together in grammatically complete ways; and provide page numbers (of print sources) in parentheses after the quotation marks but before the final punctuation of the sentence.

With the proper symbols, you can add, replace, or delete words within quoted material and enjoy considerable flexibility in the way you use quotations. In general, try to keep your use of quotations as straightforward and uncomplicated as you can. Your reader should always be able to tell what has been taken verbatim from a source and what you have done to change the material. Next are a few more suggestions for punctuating quotations within your work.

HOW SHOULD YOU PUNCTUATE QUOTATIONS?

INTRODUCING A QUOTATION

If you are introducing a quotation with a grammatically complete statement (an independent clause), follow the opening with a colon.

> When students first approach writing a research paper, their reactions often resemble Mr. Kurtz's dying words in Conrad's *Heart of Darkness*: "The horror! The horror!" (72).

A colon is the proper punctuation mark only if what precedes the colon is grammatically complete. What follows the colon may be a word, a phrase, a sentence, or even a paragraph.

Use a comma if what you are quoting is a complete sentence but your introduction to it makes the quotation itself the necessary object of a verb.

> He said, "I never met her before that occasion."

In this sentence, the verb "said" requires an object (in this case the quotation itself). "He said" is grammatically incomplete, so it is followed by a comma, not a colon. Rephrased as a complete sentence, the introductory phrase requires a colon.

His denial was emphatic: "I never met her before that occasion."

When you quote single words or phrases from an author, your punctuation should be exactly the same as if the quotation marks were not there. Don't insert unnecessary commas. As I did above, when I wrote that Nick called Gatsby's guests "moths," you should simply use the quoted word without any preceding comma.

ENDING A QUOTATION

At the end of a quoted passage, you should provide whatever end punctuation serves your grammatical needs. If you stop quoting from a passage that ends with a punctuation mark, you may drop the original punctuation mark and provide whatever is grammatically appropriate within your text. In American usage, commas and periods are always placed *inside* the final set of quotation marks, unless you provide a page number in parentheses after the quotation. Note the difference in the two following examples:

Throughout the novel, Nick refers to Gatsby's guests as "moths."

When Nick first describes Gatsby's parties, he calls the guests "moths" (39).

The page number in parentheses is not part of the quotation, so it is placed outside the quotation marks, but it is part of the sentence, so it precedes the final period. Semicolons, colons, question marks, and exclamation points always appear *outside* the final quotation marks (unless the question mark or exclamation is part of the quotation).

PRESENTING QUOTATIONS WITHIN QUOTATIONS

When you quote a passage that itself uses quotation marks, change the author's original double quotation marks to single ones to indicate a quotation within a quotation.

Original (from page 7 of Rachel Carson's *The Silent Spring*):
Since the mid-1940s over 200 basic chemicals have been created for use in killing insects, weeds, rodents, and other organisms described in the modern vernacular as "pests"; and they are sold under several thousand different brand names.

Your use of the material:
According to Rachel Carson, more than 200 chemicals are used to kill "organisms described in the modern vernacular as 'pests'" (7).

Notice that the original double quotation marks are changed to single ones to distinguish them from the ones you've provided. Because the quoted passage is presented in the text, instead of being set off in block format, the page number is placed outside the quotation marks but before the period. If no page number were provided, the final period would be placed inside *both* sets of closing quotation marks.

PUNCTUATING TITLES

Whenever you provide the title of a work, you should punctuate it properly. Titles of long works, originally published independently, should be italicized (or underlined if you are using a typewriter). Titles of novels, magazines, plays, books, television shows, films, and speeches are all italicized (or underlined). Titles of essays, short poems, short songs, articles, episodes from a television series, and short stories are all placed in quotation marks.

QUOTING POETRY

One final situation needs explanation here: quoting lines of poetry. One important difference between poetry and prose is that lines of poetry are usually shorter than the full printed width of the paper. The line breaks are an important feature of the poem's form. Thus, if you are quoting a section of a poem that, in the original, runs onto another line, you should indicate where the line ends by providing a spaced slash mark where the break occurs. For example, the opening sentence in Adrienne Rich's "Diving into the Wreck" reads (on page 22),

> First having read the book of myths,
> and loaded the camera,
> and checked the edge of the knife-blade,
> I put on
> the body-armor of black rubber
> the absurd flippers
> the grave and awkward mask.

If you wish to quote the entire sentence, present it in block format, as I did above, preserving all of the original spacing and line breaks (without slash marks). If you wish to quote fewer than three lines, present them as part of your regular paragraph (not in block format), but provide slash marks to show where her original lines were broken, as in the following example:

> In her poem "Diving into the Wreck," Adrienne Rich assumes that our history of the past is a largely fictionalized "book of myths," a metaphoric place that is dangerous for the female explorer because historians have traditionally neglected the actions of women in their accounts of our past. To document what really occurred in history, she "loaded the camera" to record the events, she "checked the edge of the knife-blade" that she might need to protect herself or to pry beneath superficial appearances, and she put on "the body-armor of black rubber / the absurd flippers / the grave and awkward mask" (22). To Rich, exploring the past is a dangerous but valuable enterprise that requires much preparation.

This paragraph illustrates much of the same selection and introduction of the quoted material that I discussed earlier. The relevant phrases have all been grammatically worked into the author's own phrasing, so that all the words, quoted and original, produce grammatical and coherent sentences. When the quoted lines break in the original, those breaks have been marked with spaced slash marks. Marking such breaks in this fashion is important only in quoting lines of poetry within your regular text, and failure to do so ignores an important feature of the original poem.

QUOTATION MARKS AND OTHER PUNCTUATION

Below are some more examples that illustrate a variety of punctuation circumstances.

A semicolon following a quotation:
Nick calls Gatsby's guests "moths"; perhaps he is not so impartial after all.

A colon following a quotation:
Emma cited several reasons for what she called her "unrestrained rage": Cathy's arrogance, Tom's indifference, and Jackie's boredom.

A quotation with an exclamation point and parenthetical page number:
The technician said, "That lapse in procedure is inexcusable!" (16).

A quotation with an exclamation point followed by attribution:
"That lapse in procedure is inexcusable!" said the technician (16).

A quoted question:
The task force sought to answer one question: "Why did the bridge collapse?"

Quoted phrases that are part of a question you ask:
How can reviewers possibly call the film *Titanic* "a passionate love story" (Ansen) and commend its "haunting tale of human nature" (Maslin)?

HOW SHOULD YOU SELECT AND CITE ELECTRONIC AND INTERNET SOURCES?

The World Wide Web and the proliferation of other electronic and online resources have made information more readily available than ever before. But the variety of such materials has also greatly increased the need for you to critically assess the information you find. The ease with which you can surf from site to site, click on links, shrink and open new windows, and cut and paste information to notepads or to documents—this rapid movement from source to source practically *encourages* sloppy and unethical uses of copyrighted information and wording. The format of the Web creates the dangerous illusion that the items you find on it are free and/or public property, akin to common knowledge that isn't owned by an author. Unlike printed material in a library, the information on an electronic source is subject to frequent change, and if you haven't been careful to copy all of the information you will need at the time you see it (or better yet, printed a hard copy of the page), you might lose your access to it, if the text has been revised. A Web page might not even list an author's name, and a particular page to which you might have been linked might not present any publishing information or context for the material on your screen. Browsing the Web seems like—and often *is*—a form of leisurely entertainment, and your habits during recreation can have dire consequences if they spill over into your writing and suspend the careful sorts of critical thinking and responsible note-taking that are essential to responsible professional and academic writing. Further, the visual similarities among different kinds of documents, when all are filtered through a browser or computer, tend to blur distinctions among them, to make them all seem equal in their reliability or authority. But there are extreme differences among the kinds of material you can view online. Despite all of these challenges, you can learn to sort the nonsense and idiocy from the truly relevant and reputable, and you can use the information with the same scrutiny and care that persuasive writers learn to apply to all that they read.

Much of the early praise for the potential of the Internet focused on the freedom of access to it as a means of publishing—as if the Internet represented the full realization of a democracy in which all people could publish and read virtually everything. At a local level, that freedom takes the form of policies of many Internet service providers that grant all subscribers some space on the server to launch their own Web sites. In effect, anyone who subscribes to an Internet hookup may post information.

One practical effect of this accessibility is that the millions of documents and images available from a terminal represent a complete mix of wholly valuable and reputable information with information that is biased, deceptive, or totally unimportant. With careful attention to the source, meticulous critical assessment of evidence and authority, and some detective work, you may find highly useful and credible information related to your topic. For example, major newspapers, magazines, and news organizations usually have Web sites—often electronic editions of or supplements to their publications and broadcasts. When you know the agency or organization that hosts the site, and the site has been assembled with the same care and editorial standards as the organization's other work, you may rely on the Web site with as much confidence as you would the print publication or broadcast.

Intermixed with online journals are countless commercial sites, individuals' Web pages, university sites, government sites, nonprofit agency pages, and highly varied other electronic forums for exchange of information. A United States government electronic archive of Senate hearings might be a click or two away from a child's hobby page. Readings posted on the Web by a professor might seem to blend seamlessly with essays written by her students. Always consider the source. The nature of your topic will assist you in determining if a particular site is relevant to your project.

SOURCE RELIABILITY: A SAMPLE TOPIC

An example will illustrate a few of the challenges involved in assessing the reliability of Web sites. Suppose you are writing an essay on the merger of two oil companies, BP Amoco and Atlantic Richfield Company (ARCO), proposed in early 2000. Entering the name of either corporation in any of the large Internet search engines (*Yahoo*, for example) will yield links to many related sites. The sheer variety of them should suggest that you need to choose a highly precise focus to make the topic manageable in an essay. That proposed merger involved issues of monopoly and antitrust legislation (the Federal Trade Commission's work), natural resource preservation, the international oil market, national security, electoral politics (because it's so controversial), ecological effects (themselves a varied lot), and a host of issues related to northern Alaska (a prominent source of oil), to name but a few. If your topic is any one of these, you will need to sift through contentious and contradictory claims by the involved parties: the corporations themselves, the political figures (national and state), interest groups (on both sides), scientists, economists, lawyers, and environmentalists. Many of these sources will simply be too biased by self-interest to serve as reputable authorities. But if your essay focuses on the conduct of the arguments themselves, on the *rhetoric* of the debate, then virtually any of these sources could become primary material. The language and argument employed by various parties would become your topic as they illustrate various techniques of argument and propaganda.

A fifteen-minute search of the topic reveals that the proposed merger intensified debate about the environmental effects of both corporations' work in northern Alaska. Both BP Amoco and ARCO discuss their environmental conduct on their Web sites. So do the Natural Resources Defense Council (NRDC) and at least two Alaskan nonprofit public-interest groups. Of course, both BP Amoco and ARCO are concerned with public relations and maximizing profits. Predictably, their sites downplay the potential environmental dangers of developing oilfields and discuss each corporation's environmental and philanthropic initiatives. BP Amoco offers several pages that celebrate Alaskan beauty and biodiversity, declaring its environmental goal: "no accidents, no harm to people, and no damage to the environment" ("BP's Commitment"). ARCO's site claims that its "extended-reach drilling" minimizes "the footprint and the environmental impact of the development" ("Alaska"). These views contrast sharply with those of the NRDC. On its site, the NRDC claims that BP Amoco was responsible for over one hundred oil spills and that it "pled guilty to a federal felony charge stemming from illegal dumping of hazardous waste at one of its Arctic fields, resulting in criminal and civil penalties of $22 million" ("Arctic National Wildlife Refuge"). The NRDC adds that ARCO's "Prudhoe Bay toxic waste pits were leaking for years into fragile tundra wetlands and wildlife habitat until an NRDC lawsuit forced the company to clean up its pollution and pay a $1 million fine" ("Arctic National Wildlife Refuge"). The specificity of the NRDC's claims and the references to events that could be verified (or not) by other sources give some credibility to the NRDC view. But we should remember that the NRDC, a national, nonprofit environmental organization, is nonetheless engaged in fundraising of its own and public relations. That the NRDC has opposed ARCO in litigation doesn't by itself call its credibility into question—but it is important. All views by interested parties should be subject to scrutiny, held to high standards of argument and use of evidence.

Further searching leads to sites by organizations with names that suggest they might offer more objective and detached views of the potential environmental impact of the merger. One such organization, located in Anchorage, calls itself the Alliance, a seemingly neutral name that nonetheless should make us ask, an alliance of *whom?* Its Web site explains that it is a "nonprofit statewide trade organization representing nearly 350 businesses, organizations, and individuals that derive their livelihood from providing products and services to oil, gas, and other natural resource exploration and development" ("Our Mission"). An organization of businesses and people in the oil industry will likely offer a perspective similar to that of BP Amoco and ARCO. It is therefore not surprising to find that the organization presents its Arctic Green Star award for environmentally sound practices to various oil companies, including ARCO. It explains, "Not only do such practices generate goodwill among the public, but they also could mean the difference between securing a contract, or losing out to a competitor who already has a record of environmental responsibility" ("Arctic Green Star Program"). This site recommends environmentally responsible corporate behavior primarily as a means of practicing good public relations and improving a corporation's chances of getting more contracts.

The Alaska Public Interest Research Group also sounds as if it would be independent of any of the key players in the dispute about the merger. Its Web site proclaims its main purpose:

> to educate citizens to enable them to participate in the political process, provide the public with practical and cost efficient ways to work with government and the private sector, and encourage and provide information to grassroots efforts that advocate for the public interest. ("About AkPIRG")

AkPIRG's site includes links to various pages about the BP Amoco and ARCO merger. One link presents AkPIRG's own view, in language that reveals its stance: "BP Whitewashes ARCO Takeover with 'White Papers.'" Another linked page offers the views by an "independent oil analyst," Richard Fineberg. AkPIRG's site may or may not represent a more balanced and documented view than the Alliance's. That would be up to you to determine with meticulous attention to the sorts of evidence provided in these documents and to the overall validity of the reasoning employed in them. Further, you should compare the arguments and evidence from all perspectives and attempt to verify the information from additional sources, ideally major news organizations, print publications (ones without economic ties to the interested parties), government documents, and court reports. As this sample topic illustrates, you should be cautious and skeptical of all printed claims—doubly so when the source is online.

CITING INTERNET WEB SITES

Citing paraphrased or quoted information from Internet sources requires some adaptation of your usual procedures. If you know the name of the author or of the organization, name it in your text as you introduce the material, mentioning the publication medium as you do so (Web site, CD-ROM, electronic journal, and so forth). If you are using a particular page from a Web site, place the title of the page in quotation marks in parentheses at the end of the sentence. Titles of pages or sections within sites are often quite long, and quoting them in your text in their entirety would be cumbersome. In such cases, you need to preserve the first word of the section name (to enable your readers to easily identify it among your list of works cited) and then use an abbreviated or shortened form that refers to the full citation at the end of the paper. Writing an abbreviated title isn't always a simple matter. For example, an underlined link on the NRDC main page is entitled "Protect the Arctic National Wildlife Refuge." The page itself, if you click on that link, is headed "Parks, Forests & Wildlands: Wilderness Preservation: In Brief: News" with another heading, "Arctic National Wildlife Refuge." In this case, the best thing might be simply to use "Arctic National Wildlife Refuge," as I do above, making certain that the actual full citation is clear in your list of works cited. The format for listing Web pages and sites will differ according to the appropriate style manual for your discipline. And, because the kinds of sources continue to evolve, most of the style manuals offer only provisional guidance and admit that the guidelines will be changing as the media evolve. But all the formats require that your final list include the author or organization (if known), the title of the page, the complete URL (Universal Resource Locator), the latest date that the page was updated (if known), and the date you actually consulted it.

It's not always easy to tell who the author is, and you might not find a date that the document was last revised. It's often tricky to decide whether a title should be presented as a part of a whole (and placed in quotation marks) or as a site on its own (and underlined or italicized). Given these uncertainties, it is doubly important to make certain that you do two things:

1. Type the complete URL with totally accurate transcription of every symbol (including slash marks and underlines) as it appears in the location box of your browser. If it is so long that you must break the line, do so only *after* one of the slash marks. The Modern Language Association (MLA) asks that you enclose the URL in angle brackets, < >, to clearly signify its status.

2. Make certain that you provide the date you consulted the site. Below are a few citations as they would appear in a list of works cited in MLA format.

A reference to a Web site:
Arctic Monitoring and Assessment Programme (AMAP) Homepage. March 1999. 9 August 2000 <http://www.grida.no/amap/>.

A reference to one page from a site:
Arctic Monitoring and Assessment Programme. "About AMAP." March
1999. 9 August 2000 <http://www.grida.no/amap/about.htm>.

**A reference to one page from a site that does not provide the date of the
last update:**
Natural Resources Defense Council. "Arctic National Wildlife Refuge." 3
August 2000 <http://www.nrdc.org/land/wilderness/arctic.asp>.

OTHER ELECTRONIC SOURCES

Your computer might be linked to some databases to which your university or
employer subscribes. Because you gain access to these databases with your
Internet browser, they might seem like ordinary Web sites, but they are actually quite distinct from the Internet. One such database is Lexis-Nexis Academic Universe, frequently available on campuses. Lexis-Nexis offers search-
able, computerized archives of published documents. This powerful—and
expensive—service is a highly useful means of gaining access to electronic versions of materials originally published in a variety of media: newspapers, magazines, journals, newsletters, trade publications, and abstracts. Lexis-Nexis
enables you to view and print information directly from your computer without the need to find the printed source in a library. It provides the actual written texts from the original sources but without the graphics, visual layout, and
pagination of the originals. Generally believed to be reputably edited and re-
liable texts, the items found on Lexis-Nexis are really distinct versions of the
original works. The service does provide the full publication information for
the items, but it reformats the document in ways that do not enable you to tell
on which page in the document a given sentence or paragraph appears. Because the item has been significantly reformatted from its original form, you
must cite the version you consulted, indicating that the material was obtained
through Lexis-Nexis. Presumably, the actual words have been transcribed accurately by the editors, but the authority for the accuracy of that transcription
now resides at Lexis-Nexis. Your citation should indicate that the online service owns the version you consulted and that what you cite is at one stage of
remove from the original printed text.

When consulting such an archive, you need to make yourself familiar with how it works—both with how the search engine enables you to make choices among dates and kinds of materials and with how the service organizes and labels the parts of the original citation. The author's name might be called the "byline"; the title of an article might be called the "headline." The services offer guidance and tips that enable you to figure out how the original citation would be reconstructed from what they provide, and most include a link to some sample citations following various formats. When you cite in your regular text a source obtained through one of these services, use the author's name (if available) or the title, as you would if you were citing the original version. This reference, whether explicit or parenthetical, should clearly identify to which item in your list of works cited the name refers. Unless the service provides the original page numbers, you do not provide them. In your list of works cited, begin by citing the work as you would the original, and then follow it by noting the name of the online service, the name of the institution that subscribed to that service and its location, the date you found the source on the site, and the URL for the site in angle brackets. Consult the appropriate style manual for your discipline for the exact way of listing such a source. If you've found an item on a service such as Lexis-Nexis and have not consulted the original version, you must acknowledge the online source. Below are two examples in MLA format (the reviews I quote above).

> Ansen, David et al. "Our Titanic Love Affair." Rev. of *Titanic*, dir. James Cameron. *Newsweek* 23 Feb. 1998: 58. Lexis-Nexis Academic Universe. Denison University, Granville, Ohio. 4 August 2000 <http://web.lexis-nexis.com/universe/>.

> Maslin, Janet. "A Spectacle as Sweeping as the Sea." Rev. of *Titanic*, dir. James Cameron. *New York Times* 19 Dec. 1997, late ed.: E1. Lexis-Nexis Academic Universe. Denison University, Granville, Ohio. 4 August 2000 <http://web.lexis-nexis.com/universe/>.

Don't despair if at first all of these rules seem complicated. Much of this material is probably review, and all of it will become second nature to you with practice. The procedures for quoting and paraphrasing are vitally important, even if they strike you at first as merely cosmetic or surface details.

Following these conventions will reassure your readers that you are ethical, competent, and careful. And if all of the papers you write are put in proper form before you turn them in, you free your professor to comment on the substance of what you say—things that probably both of you find more interesting. After all, your professor has only a limited amount of space and time to devote to commenting on your writing, and if your paper is in poor form, you waste valuable time that could be spent on more interesting matters.

Keep this handbook and refer to it whenever your memory of these conventions fades. On the final page, I've provided a brief checklist. You should consult it while revising papers that employ quoted or paraphrased material.

A FURTHER
NOTE ABOUT STYLE
MANUALS

If you are a beginning college writer and have not yet chosen a major, it doesn't make sense for you to purchase the standard style manual for every course you take in different fields. Most writing handbooks include enough information about the major style manuals to suffice in introductory classes. Once you are committed to a field of study, however, it is important for you to purchase the style manual that your professor or advisor recommends for that field. You will discover that many of the features of manuscript form, some of the features of writing style, and the format for both in-text citations and lists of references at the end of a work differ from one field to the next in significant ways. Learning to apply the guidelines for your field is part of learning the field. It might seem as if the differences from one field to the next are tiny, and they might seem arbitrary or merely a matter of a teacher's preference. But the guidelines are not, in fact, arbitrary. They reflect the values and methods of inquiry characteristic of the discipline to which they apply. For example, when formats in the social sciences seem to emphasize the year of publication, it makes sense because the recentness of information in the natural sciences typically matters more than it might in the humanities. If the natural sciences are meticulous about citing all the authors of a multi-author work, it makes sense because so many research projects involve collaborative or team efforts. You might not always know the reasons for features of the prescribed formats, but your work will appear more mature and professional if you care about and apply the guidelines in the appropriate style manual.

Below are some sample citations, included here only to illustrate a few of the differences among some prominent styles.

An article in a weekly magazine

MLA (*MLA Handbook for Writers of Research Papers*)
Strouse, Jean. "The Unknown J. P. Morgan." *The New Yorker* 29 March 1999: 66–79.

CMS (*Chicago Manual of Style*)
Strouse, Jean. "The Unknown J. P. Morgan." *The New Yorker*, 29 March 1999, 66–79.

CBE (*Scientific Style and Format*)
Strouse J. 1999 March 29. The unknown J. P. Morgan. New Yorker: 66–79.

APA (*Publication Manual of the American Psychological Association*)
Strouse, J. (1999, March 29). The Unknown J. P. Morgan. *The New Yorker*, 66–79.

APSA (*Style Manual for Political Science*)
Strouse, Jean. 1999. "The Unknown J. P. Morgan." *The New Yorker*, March 29: 66–79.

A book

MLA

Brooks, David. *Bobos in Paradise: The New Upper Class and How They Got There.* New York: Simon & Schuster, 2000.

CMS

Brooks, David. *Bobos in Paradise: The New Upper Class and How They Got There.* New York: Simon & Schuster, 2000.

CBE

Brooks D. 2000. Bobos in paradise: the new upper class and how they got there. New York: Simon & Schuster. 284 p.

APA

Brooks, D. (2000). *Bobos in Paradise: The New Upper Class and How They Got There*. New York: Simon & Schuster.

APSA

Brooks, David. 2000. *Bobos in Paradise: The New Upper Class and How They Got There*. New York: Simon & Schuster.

A Web site

MLA

Sierra Club Home page. Sierra Club. 6 August 2001 <http://www.sierraclub.org/>.

CMS

Sierra Club. Sierra Club home page. 2001. <http://www.sierraclub.org/> (6 August 2001).

CBE

Sierra Club. 2001. Sierra Club home page. <http://www.sierraclub.org/>. Accessed 2001 Aug. 6.

APA

Sierra Club. (2001). Sierra Club Home page. Retrieved August 6, 2001 from the World Wide Web: http://www.sierraclub.org/

APSA

Sierra Club. 2001. Sierra Club Home Page. http://www.sierraclub.org/ (accessed Aug. 6, 2001).

REVISION
CHECKLIST FOR
QUOTING AND
PARAPHRASING

1. Are all of your paragraphs developed adequately, with evidence for your argument or illustration of your complex ideas? Is the paragraph primarily your words, with quotations or paraphrased evidence serving only as supporting material? Do you provide too much information from sources, or too little?

2. If you have paraphrased, did you introduce the material from your source to indicate clearly what is from the source? Did you mention the author? Did you provide a note or a parenthetical citation of the source so that your readers would have all the information they need to locate the source and page from which the information comes?

3. Is the wording of paraphrased material entirely your own? Does it accurately reflect the viewpoint expressed in the original?

4. If you quote, have you introduced each passage, or does your context make it clear that the words are quoted from a source? Have you followed the quotation with a page number or with a note? Is each quoted passage introduced sufficiently so that quoted words fit together grammatically with your own, to ensure that your reader will understand the significance of the passage?

5. Are quoted words in proper form? Are they quoted accurately and marked by quotation marks? Have any added words or letters been placed in square brackets, and have deleted words been replaced by an

ellipsis? Have you indicated the line breaks in quoted poetry with slash marks? Have you punctuated the quotations properly?

6. Have you followed all quotations, particularly longer, block quotations, with your own analysis or interpretation of the passages? Are the transitions to and from quoted material smooth and coherent?

7. In your citations of Web sites, have you made certain that the URL is typed correctly and provided the date that you consulted the source?

8. If you've consulted sources that have been indexed and re-presented by an online database, have you noted the online version that you have cited?

9. Have you followed the format for citations required by the style manual that is used in your discipline? Do all of your citations present all of the necessary information about the works you consulted?

APPENDIX:
INTERNET RESOURCES

This section presents useful Web sites organized by disciplines within the humanities and social sciences. Some of these sites provide resources for research within a discipline, and some provide guides for writing papers and citing sources. Each discipline has its own resources and its own rules, so these sites provide an introduction to these resources and rules. They barely scratch the surface of what's available on the Internet, but they should provide a good start.

Anthropology

Anthropology in the News
Contains the latest findings throughout anthropology. Maintained by Texas A&M University.
http://www.tamu.edu/anthropology/news.html

Anthropology Resources on the Internet
General guide to online anthropology resources from around the world.
http://home.worldnet.fr/~clist/Anthro/index.html

Archaeology on the Net
General guide to archaeology resources on the Internet.
http://www.serve.com/archaeology/main.html

WWW Virtual Library: Anthropology
General anthropology resource with links for each subdiscipline within anthropology.
  http://vlib.anthrotech.com/

Communication

College of Communication at Boston University
This online journal, maintained by the University of Boston, contains resources for
  all subdisciplines within the study of communication.
  http://www.bu.edu/com/communication.html

EraM—Ethnicity, Racism, and Media Discussion Forum
This site explores the issues surrounding ethnicity, racism, and the media.
  http://www.code1.com/cybercolonies/eram/index.htm

National Press Club
This is a general resource site for journalists in all media formats.
  http://npc.press.org/

National Speakers Association
Resources for speakers, whether professional or amateur.
  http://www.nsaspeaker.org/

netMEDIA by GO PUBLIC
Links to media organizations around the world.
  http://www.go-public.com/netmedia/

Penn State University Library's History of the Book and Printing
Resources for print media, including a history of the book. Maintained by the Penn
  State Library.
  http://www.libraries.psu.edu/crsweb/select/sxh/hisbk.htm

RobertNiles.com—Journalism and Online Publishing Help
Basic stats for journalists or other laypersons.
  http://www.robertniles.com/

Society of Professional Journalists
The Society of Professional Journalists is the nation's largest and most broad-based
  journalism organization.
  http://spj.org/

Toastmasters International
Tips for making speeches put together by Toastmasters International.
  http://www.toastmasters.org/tips.htm

Geography

Calgeog Resources: Cultural Geography
Cultural Geography Web resources. Maintained by California State University–Santa Barbara.
  http://cgs.csusb.edu/cultural.html

CU Department of Geography—Geography Resource Center
General resources for geography. Maintained by the University of Colorado.
  http://www.colorado.edu/geography/virtdept/resources/contents.htm

Internet Resources for Geography and Geology
General resources for geography and geology. Maintained by the University of Wisconsin–Stevens Point.
  http://www.uwsp.edu/geo/internet/geog_geol_resources.html

Map Projections Poster
Map projections resources maintained by the U.S. Geological Survey.
  http://mac.usgs.gov/mac/isb/pubs/MapProjections/projections.html

Maps and Cartography
Earth Science and Map Library Map Collection at the University of California, Berkeley.
  http://www.lib.berkeley.edu/EART/MapCollections.html

Research Guide–Geography
Geography research guide with both resources for research and tips for references and citation styles.
  http://www.lwc.edu/administrative/library/geograph.htm

History

HISTORY
General resources for history organized by historical time period.
  http://www.scholiast.org/history/

Horus' History Links
General resources for the history discipline. Maintained by the University of California, Riverside history faculty.
  http://www.ucr.edu/h-gig/horuslinks.html

How to Read a Primary Source
Guide to reading and interpreting primary sources. Very helpful for researchers.
  http://www.bowdoin.edu/~prael/writing_guides/primary.htm

Welcome to History and Theory
This Web site and online journal is devoted to exploring the links between philosophy and history.
http://www.historyandtheory.org/

Women's Biographies: Distinguished Women of Past and Present
This site is devoted to the history of women throughout the world.
http://www.DistinguishedWomen.com/

WWW Virtual Library for History
General resource with links to many history resources. Maintained by the University of Kansas.
http://history.cc.ukans.edu/history/WWW_history_main.html

Philosophy

Descartes' Meditations Home Page
This site contains an online edition of Descartes' classic work of philosophical reflections.
http://philos.wright.edu/DesCartes/Meditations.html

Ethics Updates Home Page
This site contains resources on the following topics: moral theory, relativism, pluralism, religion, egoism.
http://ethics.acusd.edu/

Philosophers: Main Page
This site provides easy access to resources in philosophy, categorized by philosopher.
http://www.epistemelinks.com/Main/MainPers.asp

PHILOSOPHY COMIX
This site contains examples of philosophical topics from contemporary comic strips.
http://members.aol.com/lshauser/phlcomix.html

Philosophy in Cyberspace
This is an excellent source of philosophy resources on the Web broken down into subtopics.
http://www-personal.monash.edu.au/~dey/phil/index.htm

Philosophy Pages
This site focuses on Web links to Western philosophy sites.
http://www.philosophypages.com/index.htm

Philosophy, Introduction
This site provides a general overview of what philosophy is.
http://pespmc1.vub.ac.be/PHILOSI.html

Political Science

Inter-University Consortium for Political and Social Research Web Site
This site contains social science data and resources for researchers.
http://www.icpsr.umich.edu/

Political Science Internet Resources
This site contains hundreds of links to political science resources. Organized by subdiscipline. Maintained by Western Connecticut State University.
http://www.wcsu.edu/socialsci/polscres.html

Social Science Research Resources
This site is a guide to social science research resources. Maintained by the University
of Colorado.
http://socsci.colorado.edu/POLSCI/RES/research.html

WWW Resources for Political Scientists
This site contains links to political science resources organized by topic and type of
resource. Maintained by the University of Colorado.
http://osiris.colorado.edu/POLSCI/links.html

Sociology

American Sociological Association Manuscript Checklist
http://asanet.org/pubs/notice.pdf

Classical Sociological Theory
This site contains online texts of classical social thinkers. Maintained by the University of Chicago.
http://www.spc.uchicago.edu/ssr1/PRELIMS/theory.html

Research Methods Tutorials
Students at Cornell University have put together this site with lessons that include
sampling, field research multivariate analysis, and analysis of variance techniques.
http://trochim.human.cornell.edu/tutorial/TUTORIAL.HTM

Social Science Hub
Excellent starting point for research. Comprehensive enough to include many of the
major categories within the discipline.
http://www.sshub.com/

Sociology Online
This British site for all students of sociology, criminology, and social thought is full of
information about both classical and contemporary thinkers.
http://www.sociologyonline.co.uk/

SocioSite
This site, maintained by the University of Amsterdam, provides a global perspective on
sociology with access to a number of European theorists.
http://www.pscw.uva.nl/sociosite/topics/sociologists.html

UCLA Statistics Textbook
This site provides a helpful statistics resource.
http://ebook.stat.ucla.edu/textbook/

Voice of the Shuttle: Cultural Studies Page
This site has references to a wide range of current sociological thinkers, many specif-
ically oriented toward cultural theories.
http://vos.ucsb.edu/shuttle/cultural.html

WORKS CITED

The Alaska Public Interest Research Group (AkPIRG). "About AkPIRG." 3 August 2000. <http://www.akpirg.org/about/aboutAKPIRG.html>.

——. "BP Whitewashes ARCO Takeover with 'White Papers.'" Press Advisory 25 October 1999. 3 August 2000. <http://www.akpirg/org/campaigns/bp/9910BPpress conf991025.html>.

——. "From the Desk of Richard A. Fineburg." 3 August 2000. <http://www.akpirg/org/campaigns/bp/9910BPceraRAFfinal.html>.

The Alliance. "Arctic Green Star Program." 3 August 2000. <http://www.akalliance.org/programs.htm>.

——. "Our Mission." 3 August 2000. <http://www.akalliance.org/abouthe.htm>.

Ansen, David et al. "Our Titanic Love Affair." Rev. of *Titanic*, dir. James Cameron. *Newsweek* 23 Feb. 1998: 58. Lexis-Nexis Academic Universe. Denison University, Granville, Ohio. 4 August 2000. <http://web.lexis-nexis.com/universe/>.

ARCO. "Alaska." 3 August 2000. <http://www.arco.com/world/no_amer/expl_prod_ala.html>.

B.P. Amoco. "BP's Commitment to Health, Safety and the Environment." 11 August 2000. <http://www.bp.com/alive/performance/health_safety_and_environment_performance/>.

Carson, Rachel. *The Silent Spring*. Cambridge, Mass.: Riverside Press, 1962.

Conrad, Joseph. *Heart of Darkness*. Ed. Robert Kimbrough. 3rd ed. New York: W. W. Norton & Company, 1988.

Fitzgerald, F. Scott. *The Great Gatsby*. New York: Charles Scribner's Sons, 1925.

Lambert, Craig. "Desperately Seeking Summa." *Harvard Magazine* May–June 1993: 36–40.

Maslin, Janet. "A Spectacle as Sweeping as the Sea." Rev. of *Titanic*, dir. James Cameron. *New York Times* 19 Dec. 1997, late ed.: E1. Lexis-Nexis Academic Universe. Denison University, Granville, Ohio. 4 August 2000. <http://web.lexis-nexis.com/universe/>.

Natural Resources Defense Council. "Arctic National Wildlife Refuge." 3 August 2000. <http://www.nrdc.org/land/wilderness/arctic.asp>.

Quinn, Carin C. "The Jeaning of America—and the World." *American Heritage* Apr./May 1978: 14–21.

Rich, Adrienne. *Diving into the Wreck: Poems 1971–1972*. New York: W. W. Norton & Company, 1973.

NOTES

NOTES

NOTES

NOTES

NOTES

NOTES